THE ULTIMATE
NEW ENGLAND PATRIOTS
TRIVIA BOOK

A Collection of Amazing Trivia Quizzes
and Fun Facts for Die-Hard Patriots Fans!

D1114623

Ray Walker

Exclusive Free Book

Crazy Sports Stories

As a thank you for getting a copy of this book I would like to offer you a free copy of my book Crazy Sports Stories which comes packed with interesting stories from your favorite sports such as Football, Hockey, Baseball, Basketball and more.

Grab your free copy over at
RayWalkerMedia.com/Bonus

CONTENTS

INTRODUCTION

The New England Patriots have made their fans, worldwide, proud ever since joining the American Football League in 1960 as the Boston Patriots and then the New England Patriots, renamed in 1971 after relocating to Foxborough, Massachusetts, following the 1970 merger of the AFL and NFL.

Patriots fans have loved their team through the worst of seasons, knowing that New England would become a winner one day. Supporters have been entertained by players who will go down in history as some of the best to play the sport and others whose names are unrecognizable to football fans outside of Patriots country.

This book will be a celebration of the best and worst times of the last 60 years, from the Patriots' first preseason game on July 30, 1960, to its loss in the 2019 American Football Conference (AFC) playoffs. Along the way, the franchise has become one of the NFL's best, and under the tutelage of head coach Bill Belichick, has become an NFL dynasty as well.

This book is a celebration of the New England Patriots. It includes all the interesting, important details that help football fans understand more about the players that have worn the

Patriots uniform with pride. Each chapter in the book has twenty questions mixed between multiple choice, true and false, with answers located on a separate page, and a "Did You Know?" section containing important data about the Patriots.

Enjoy the book by testing yourself with the quiz questions to see how much Patriots history you know. Or, if you choose, use the book as a competitive tool in wagering with friends or other sports fans to see how you stack up and see who can claim the title as the biggest Patriots fan.

If you want to learn more about the New England Patriots, this book is an excellent tool to gain more knowledge into how the team developed into one of the biggest dynasties in NFL history, if not the biggest. Regardless of how you decide to use this book, rest assured the information, records, and individual and team statistics are up to date through the 2020 NFL Draft.

New England is transitioning in 2020, but Patriots fans know their team will topple more records and add more awards to their trophy cases with each season's passing. Remember how much information you digested while reading this book the next time a friend asks you, "When did the New England Patriots join the AFL?".

CHAPTER 1:

ORIGINS & HISTORY

QUIZ TIME!

1. In what year were the New England Patriots founded?

    a. 1957

    b. 1958

    c. 1959

    d. 1960

2. What was the original name of the team?

    a. Massachusetts Patriots

    b. New England Patriots

    c. Boston Patriots

    d. Beantown Patriots

3. New England played in Fenway Park, the home of the Boston Red Sox, for some of their AFL games.

    a. True

    b. False

4. What team did the New England Patriots lose to in the 1963 AFL Championship Game?

    a. Cleveland Browns

    b. San Diego Chargers

    c. Buffalo Bills

    d. New York Jets

5. In what year did the Boston Patriots become the New England Patriots?

    a. 1965

    b. 1971

    c. 1975

    d. 1980

6. In what year did the Patriots draft Stanford quarterback, Jim Plunkett?

    a. 1970

    b. 1971

    c. 1973

    d. 1975

7. In what year did New England hire current head coach Bill Belichick?

    a. 1998

    b. 2000

    c. 2002

    d. 2005

8. In what year did the New England Patriots move to a new stadium in Foxborough?

   a. 1968
   b. 1969
   c. 1970
   d. 1971

9. In what year did the Patriots move from Foxborough Stadium to their current Gillette Stadium?

   a. 2000
   b. 2002
   c. 2004
   d. 2006

10. What year did the New England Patriots have a record of 16-0 during the NFL regular season?

   a. 2006
   b. 2007
   c. 2009
   d. 2010

11. How many seasons have the Patriots reached the playoffs under head coach Bill Belichick?

   a. 16
   b. 17
   c. 18
   d. 20

12. In what year did current owner Bob Kraft buy the New England Patriots?

    a. 1992
    b. 1993
    c. 1994
    d. 1995

13. In what year did the Patriots play in their first Super Bowl?

    a. 1985
    b. 1987
    c. 1989
    d. 1991

14. How many Super Bowls have the Patriots played in?

    a. 9
    b. 10
    c. 11
    d. 13

15. How many Super Bowls have the Patriots won?

    a. 6
    b. 7
    c. 9
    d. 10

16. In what round did the New England Patriots draft Tom Brady?

    a. 4th
    b. 5th
    c. 6th
    d. 7th

17. Who did Tom Brady replace as the starting quarterback for New England?

    a. Matt Cassell
    b. Drew Bledsoe
    c. Jim Plunkett
    d. Doug Flutie

18. Bill Parcells was the head coach for New England from 1993-1996.

    a. True
    b. False

19. How many consecutive AFC East titles have the Patriots won?

    a. 8
    b. 9
    c. 10
    d. 11

20. What team did Tom Brady sign up to play for in 2020?

    a. Buffalo Bills
    b. Dallas Cowboys
    c. Miami Dolphins
    d. Tampa Bay Buccaneers

QUIZ ANSWERS

1. C – 1959

2. C – Boston Patriots

3. A – True

4. B – San Diego Chargers

5. B – 1971

6. B – 1971

7. B – 2000

8. D – 1971

9. B – 2002

10. B – 2007

11. B – 17

12. C – 1994

13. A – 1985

14. C – 11

15. A – 6

16. C – 6th

17. B – Drew Bledsoe

18. A – True

19. D – 11

20. D – Tampa Bay Buccaneers

DID YOU KNOW?

1. The Patriots were not the first professional football team to represent the city of Boston. The Boston Bulldogs were inaugurated in 1929 and disbanded in the same year. In addition, the Boston Redskins, originally the Braves, played in Boston in 1932 but relocated to Washington, D.C., five seasons later.

2. The Patriots were victorious over the Buffalo Bills, by a score of 28-7 on July 30, 1960, in the first-ever preseason game for the American Football League.

3. In the final game the Patriots played at Alumni Stadium, the game was delayed when a popcorn machine caught fire under the bleachers, and a large portion of the crowd had to scatter for safety. No one was hurt, and following the fire, the crowd found a place to sit, and the game continued.

4. The Patriots started in 1960 as the Boston Patriots, and requested their name be changed to the Bay State Patriots in 1971, when they relocated to a new stadium in Foxborough, Massachusetts. The request was rejected when it was pointed out to the team that the team's abbreviation would be the B.S. Patriots.

5. Mark Henderson, a snowplow operator, became a Patriots hero in 1982 when he cleared an area of the playing field for the Pats' placekicker John Smith, whose subsequent

field goal late in the game defeated Miami. Henderson was working the game on a work-release program from an area prison.

6. In 1985, after going 11-5 in the regular season and reaching the postseason as a wild card selection, the Patriots made their first Super Bowl appearance. They went on to become the first team in NFL history to win three postseason games on the road but were crushed in Super Bowl XX by the Chicago Bears 46-10.

7. Tom Brady, undoubtedly one of the all-time best quarterbacks and future Hall-of-Famer, wasn't originally touted as an NFL quarterback while playing collegiate football for the Michigan Wolverines. At one point, Brady was 7th on the depth chart at Michigan and was not selected by New England until the 6th round of the 2000 NFL Draft.

8. New England trailed the Atlanta Falcons 28-3 in Super Bowl LI, but scored 25 consecutive points to push the game into overtime. The comeback was the biggest ever in Super Bowl history, and it was the first time any Super Bowl had gone to overtime.

9. New England Patriots head coach Bill Belichick is considered by football pundits to be one of the best to ever roam the sidelines. However, Belichick almost went in a different direction, calling lacrosse his favorite sport after playing both football and lacrosse in high school and college.

10. The Patriots have played in several stadiums, all within

Massachusetts, since playing their first game in 1960. In 1992 then-owner, James Orthwein, wanted to move the Patriots to his home state of Missouri and rename them the St. Louis Stallions. Foxboro Stadium owner Bob Kraft nixed the move by not allowing the Patriots to break their lease and eventually bought the team from Orthwein two years later.

CHAPTER 2:

JERSEYS & NUMBERS

QUIZ TIME!

1. What colors were the jerseys and numbers for New England between 1960-1972?

    a. Blue and white

    b. Blue and red

    c. Red and white

    d. Black and red

2. In what year did the Patriots began using their "Flying Elvis" logo?

    a. 1991

    b. 1992

    c. 1993

    d. 1994

3. In what year did the Patriots begin using navy blue jerseys?

    a. 1997

    b. 1998

c. 1999

d. 2000

4. In what season did the Patriots switch from rounded numbers back to block numbers?

    a. 2000

    b. 2001

    c. 2002

    d. 2003

5. In what season did the Patriots take part in the Color Rush program, using monochrome navy uniforms?

    a. 2014

    b. 2015

    c. 2016

    d. 2017

6. The Patriots introduced an all-white Color Rush uniform for a Thursday Night game in 2017.

    a. True

    b. False

7. What Patriots kicker wore number 1, and was named to the Pro Bowl in 1980?

    a. Tony Franklin

    b. John Smith

    c. Adam Vinatieri

    d. Stephen Gostkowski

8. What number did quarterback Steve Grogan wear for 16 seasons with the Patriots?

a. 14

b. 15

c. 16

d. 17

9. What number did Gino Cappelletti use for New England as a wide receiver and kicker?

a. 18

b. 19

c. 20

d. 21

10. What NFL Hall-of-Famer wore number 40 for the Patriots as a cornerback?

a. Mike Haynes

b. Ty Law

c. Malcolm Butler

d. Raymond Clayborn

11. What number did Drew Bledsoe wear for nine seasons as the Patriots' starting quarterback?

a. 10

b. 11

c. 12

d. 14

12. How many consecutive Pro Bowl selections did defensive end Richard Seymour earn wearing number 93?

a. 0

b. 3

c. 4

d. 5

13. Who wore number 28 for the Patriots for just three seasons, but still ranks 4th on the team's career rushing list, including rushing for 1,487 yards as a rookie?

    a. Craig James
    b. Curtis Martin
    c. Sam Cunningham
    d. Tony Collins

14. What number did Randy Moss wear for three seasons as a wide receiver for New England?

    a. 80
    b. 81
    c. 85
    d. 88

15. While wearing number 80 for the Patriots, how many Super Bowls did underrated player Troy Brown win?

    a. 1
    b. 2
    c. 3
    d. 4

16. What number did linebacker Andre Tippett, who leads the Patriots in career sacks with 100, wear during his 11 seasons with the team?

    a. 54
    b. 55

c. 56

d. 58

17. John Hannah is considered by many to be the best offensive lineman in NFL history. While wearing number 74 for 13 seasons, how many Pro Bowls was Hannah named to?

   a. 6

   b. 7

   c. 8

   d. 9

18. Who was the last player for New England to wear number 12 before Tom Brady?

   a. Tom Ramsey

   b. Mike Walker

   c. Matt Cavanaugh

   d. Eddie Wilson

19. Who is the only player to wear number 20 for the New England Patriots?

   a. Tony Collins

   b. Raymond Claiborne

   c. Craig James

   d. Gino Cappelletti

20. Who is the only player to wear number 0 for the New England Patriots?

   a. Josh Miller

   b. Zuriel Smith

   c. Tony Franklin

   d. Tony Smith

QUIZ ANSWERS

1. C – Red and white

2. 2-C – 1993

3. D – 2000

4. A – 2000

5. C – 2016

6. A – True

7. B – John Smith

8. A – 14

9. C – 20

10. A – Mike Haynes

11. B – 11

12. D – 5

13. B – Curtis Martin

14. B – 81

15. C – 3

16. C – 56

17. D – 9

18. A – Tom Ramsey

19. D – Gino Cappelletti

20. B – Zuriel Smith

DID YOU KNOW?

1. The longest-used logo by the New England Patriots on jerseys and helmets is that of a Revolutionary War Minuteman hiking the ball, used between 1961 and 1992. The Minuteman was known as "Pat Patriot," which later became the name of New England's mascot.

2. When Adrian Wilson joined New England in 2013, the 12-year veteran wanted to wear jersey number 24, but that number was already worn by Kyle Arrington. Wilson offered to buy a year's worth of diapers for Arrington, who was a father of a newborn, in exchange for the use of number 24. The two agreed, and Wilson wore number 24, while Arrington took number 25, and plenty of diapers.

3. The most recent player to wear number 1 for the Patriots was wide receiver Cameron Meredith. The only other players to wear the number since 1960 were John Smith, Tony Franklin, and Eric Schubert, all kickers.

4. Future Hall-of-Famer Tom Brady was the sixth, and most likely last, player to wear jersey number 12, donning it from 2000 through 2019. The other five players were Dan Allard, Eddie Wilson, Mike Walker, Matt Cavanaugh, and Tom Ramsey. New England will most likely retire the number in honor of Brady's accomplishments over his 20 seasons with the team.

5. Walt Cudzik, Jon Morris, and Rod Shoate all wore number

56 before Andre Tippett donned it from 1982 to 1993. Tippett was the last Patriots player to wear the number, and after being inducted into the NFL Hall of Fame in 2008, New England will most likely end up retiring the number in his honor.

6. The New England Patriots have retired just seven numbers in franchise history. The numbers are 20 (Gino Cappelletti), 40 (Mike Haynes), 57 (Steve Nelson), 73 (John Hannah), 78 (Bruce Armstrong), 79 (Jim Lee Hunt), and 89 (Bob Dee). Jersey numbers 56 (Andre Tippett) and 12 (Tom Brady) are on a short list of numbers that the Patriots will retire sooner than later.

7. The Patriots won three consecutive Super Bowl titles wearing white jerseys before their Super Bowl LII appearance against the Philadelphia Eagles. The Patriots made a request to the NFL to use their white jersey, against the Eagles, rather than the blue ones they were supposed to use. The NFL agreed, and New England went on to lose against Philadelphia.

8. Only four players have worn number 4 for the New England Patriots. The first was kicker/running back Jerrel Wilson in 1978, and the most recent Jarrett Stidham, who is expected to start at quarterback after the departure of future Hall-of-Famer Tom Brady, who signed to play with the Tampa Bay Buccaneers.

9. While inducting 27 former players into the team's Hall of Fame, New England has had just four former players

inducted into the NFL Hall of Fame, including John Hannah, Gino Cappelletti, Mike Haynes, and Andre Tippett.

10. New England announced in April 2000 that it would use, for the first time in franchise history, a monochrome uniform as its primary home uniform. In addition, the Patriots unveiled a brand new away uniform, with navy pants as the pants contrast both the home and away jerseys.

CHAPTER 3:

PATRIOTS QUARTERBACKS

QUIZ TIME!

1. Who was the first starting quarterback for the Patriots in 1960 when the team was named the Boston Patriots?
   a. Babe Parilli
   b. Butch Songin
   c. Tom Greene
   d. Tom Yewcic

2. Who was the first starting quarterback when the Patriots moved to Foxborough and became the New England Patriots?
   a. Mike Taliaferro
   b. Joe Kapp
   c. Jim Plunkett
   d. Steve Grogan

3. How many straight seasons was Steve Grogan the starting quarterback for the Patriots?
   a. 6
   b. 7

c. 8

d. 9

4. How many games did Matt Cavanaugh start at quarterback for New England in 1980 in place of Grogan?

   a. 3

   b. 4

   c. 5

   d. 6

5. Between 1987 and 1993, the Patriots did not have a permanent starting quarterback. During that time, what was the highest number of starting quarterbacks they used in a single season?

   a. 3

   b. 4

   c. 5

   d. 6

6. Who tackled quarterback Drew Bledsoe out of bounds, and injured the Patriots quarterback, opening the door for Tom Brady to become the Patriots' new starting quarterback?

   a. Mo Lewis

   b. Lawrence Taylor

   c. Joe Klecko

   d. Mark Gastineau

7. What quarterback led New England to its first Super Bowl appearance in 1986?

   a. Tony Eason

   b. Drew Bledsoe

c. Steve Grogan

d. Doug Flutie

8. Which quarterback did NOT start for New England during the 1987 regular season?

a. Marc Wilson

b. Tony Eason

c. Doug Flutie

d. Bob Bleier

9. What selection was Tom Brady picked in the 2000 NFL Draft?

a. 197th

b. 199th

c. 201st

d. 203rd

10. Tom Brady won 5 Super Bowls while playing with the New England Patriots.

a. True

b. False

11. How many times did New England reach the Super Bowl while Tom Brady was the starting quarterback?

a. 7

b. 8

c. 9

d. 10

12. Who started 15 games at quarterback for New England in 2008 after Brady was lost to a season-ending knee injury?

a. Scott Zolak

b. Matt Cassel

c. Jacoby Brissett

d. Jimmy Garoppolo

13. How many Super Bowl MVP awards has Tom Brady won?

    a. 2

    b. 3

    c. 4

    d. 5

14. Tom Brady is one of two quarterbacks in the NFL to win the Super Bowl his first season as a starter. Who is the other?

    a. Peyton Manning

    b. Eli Manning

    c. Kurt Warner

    d. Troy Aikman

15. How many games was Tom Brady suspended for in 2016 for his alleged involvement in Deflategate?

    a. 3

    b. 4

    c. 5

    d. None

16. Where did Tom Brady play college football?

    a. Michigan State

    b. Michigan

    c. Central Michigan

    d. Western Michigan

17. How many games has Tom Brady won as quarterback, through the 2019 season?

    a. 216
    b. 217
    c. 218
    d. 219

18. Tom Brady is married to what well-known fashion model?

    a. Heidi Klum
    b. Kate Upton
    c. Gisele Bündchen
    d. Adriana Lima

19. Which President of the United States invited Tom Brady as a special guest to his State of the Union Address?

    a. Donald Trump
    b. George W. Bush
    c. Bill Clinton
    d. Barack Obama

20. Which former New England teammate of Brady's has unretired and signed to play for the Tampa Bay Buccaneers?

    a. Randy Moss
    b. Rob Gronkowski
    c. Wes Walker
    d. Troy Brown

QUIZ ANSWERS

1. B – Butch Songin

2. C – Jim Plunkett

3. A – 6

4. 4- B – 4

5. 5- C – 5

6. A – Mo Lewis

7. A – Tony Eason

8. A – Marc Wilson

9. B – 199th

10. B – False

11. C – 9

12. B – Matt Cassel

13. C – 4

14. C – Kurt Warner

15. B – 4

16. B – Michigan

17. D – 219

18. C – Gisele Bündchen

19. B – George W. Bush

20. B – Rob Gronkowski

DID YOU KNOW?

1. Babe Parilli was the starting quarterback for the Patriots for six seasons from 1961 to 1967 and started 70 games. Tom Yewcic (4), Butch Songin (6), Eddie Wilson (1), and Don Trull (3) started a combined 14 games during that span but no more than 6 in any one season.

2. Jim Plunkett started every game during the regular season for New England for four straight seasons starting in 1971. Plunkett was drafted out of Stanford University, and both of his parents were blind. His mother lost her sight at 19 due to scarlet fever, and his father was legally blind from birth.

3. Tom Brady threw for 74,571 yards as quarterback for the New England Patriots from 2000 through the 2019 season. The next closest quarterback for the Patriots in passing yardage is Drew Bledsoe with 29,657, or a whopping 44,914 yards less than Brady's team record.

4. Butch Songin was the first Boston Patriots starting quarterback. Songin also played for the New York Titans and the Hamilton Tiger-Cats in what is now the Canadian Football League and was an All-American defenseman for the Boston College Eagles ice hockey team.

5. Since the Patriots started playing at Gillette Stadium in September of 2002, just four quarterbacks have started at home for New England, including Tom Brady, Matt Cassel, Jimmy Garoppolo, and Jacoby Brissett.

6. Tom Brady has started more games (283) at quarterback for New England than any other player. Steve Grogan, with 135 starts at quarterback, has the second most in New England franchise history but 148 fewer than leader Brady.

7. In 1987, the New England Patriots had five starting quarterbacks thanks to injuries and poor performance. Steven Grogan, with six starts, led the Patriots in 1987, but Tom Ramsey and Tony Eason started three games each. Bob Bleier started two, and Doug Flutie started one.

8. Tom Brady has nearly every record in franchise history for quarterbacks leading the team in most starts, overall wins, passes attempted, passes completed, total yards gained, and touchdown passes. Brady has also rushed more times than any other quarterback for the Patriots, but Steven Grogan holds the career rushing record for New England quarterbacks with 2,176 and rushing touchdowns with 35.

9. Drew Bledsoe was drafted by the New England Patriots in 1993 with the 1st overall pick and started under center his rookie season. After losing his starting job to Tom Brady due to a serious laceration to his liver, Bledsoe was traded to the Buffalo Bills, where he played three seasons, followed by two seasons with the Dallas Cowboys.

10. New England has had 28 starting quarterbacks over the history of the franchise, dating back to 1960. The most to start during one season were five in 1987. The fewest games started at quarterback for New England is one by Eddie Wilson and Tom Owen; and the most, by Brady with 283.

CHAPTER 4:

PASS RECEIVERS

QUIZ TIME!

1. Who is the all-time leading receiver for the New England Patriots in yards gained?

    a. Rob Gronkowski

    b. Troy Brown

    c. Stanley Morgan

    d. Irving Fryar

2. How many yards has Julian Edelman gained as a wide receiver for the New England Patriots?

    a. 6,345

    b. 6,507

    c. 6,765

    d. 6,943

3. What Patriots wide receiver is the all-time team leader in receptions, with 672?

    a. Wes Welker

    b. Julian Edelman

c. Troy Brown

d. Rob Gronkowski

4. What Patriots wide receiver is the all-time leader in yards per catch with an average of 20.3?

a. Stanley Morgan

b. Harold Jackson

c. Randy Moss

d. Irving Fryar

5. Wes Welker holds the all-time New England Patriots record for most receptions in one season, with how many?

a. 120

b. 122

c. 123

d. 125

6. Who holds the Patriots' single-season receiving record for yards gained at 1,569?

a. Wes Welker

b. Julian Edelman

c. Stanley Morgan

d. Randy Moss

7. What player has caught the most touchdown passes from Tom Brady, with 79?

a. Randy Moss

b. Julian Edelman

c. Wes Welker

d. Rob Gronkowski

8. Who gained 4,589 yards receiving for New England while also playing running back and kicker?

   a. Kevin Faulk
   b. Gino Cappelletti
   c. James White
   d. Jim Nance

9. What university did Stanley Morgan start with before joining the New England Patriots in 1977?

   a. Texas
   b. Tennessee
   c. Kentucky
   d. West Virginia

10. What Patriots receiver has caught the most playoff touchdowns, with 12?

   a. Randy Moss
   b. Wes Welker
   c. Troy Brown
   d. Rob Gronkowski

11. Which New England wide receiver is second in career playoff receptions, with 118?

   a. Robert Gronkowski
   b. Troy Brown
   c. Wes Welker
   d. Julian Edelman

12. In what round did the New England Patriots draft receiver Julian Edelman from the Kent State Golden Flashes?

a. 5th
b. 6th
c. 7th
d. 8th

13. Which former New England Patriots player holds the NFL record for most receptions for an undrafted wide receiver, with 903?

    a. Troy Brown
    b. Wes Welker
    c. Irving Fryar
    d. Stanley Morgan

14. Former Patriots wide receiver Troy Brown played his college career at what Conference-USA university?

    a. Middle Tennessee State Blue Raider
    b. Old Dominion Monarchs
    c. Marshall Thundering Herd
    d. Southern Mississippi Golden Eagles

15. Julian Edelman has more career receiving yards with New England than Wes Welker.

    a. True
    b. False

16. Which receiver holds the record for most touchdown receptions for the New England Patriots, with 79?

    a. Troy Brown
    b. Deion Branch
    c. Rob Gronkowski
    d. Stanley Morgan

17. Former Patriots tight end Aaron Hernandez was imprisoned and later committed suicide.

    a. True
    b. False

18. Who holds the Patriots' single-season record for most touchdown receptions, with 23?

    a. Randy Moss
    b. Rob Gronkowski
    c. Stanley Morgan
    d. Wes Walker

19. How many touchdown passes did Stanley Morgan catch while playing for the New England Patriots from 1977 through 1989?

    a. 76
    b. 77
    c. 78
    d. 67

20. What two former New England Patriots players finished tied for third in career touchdown receptions for the team, with 50?

    a. Wes Walker and Julian Edelman
    b. Irving Fryar and Stanley Morgan
    c. Ben Coates and Randy Moss
    d. Rob Gronkowski and Troy Brown

QUIZ ANSWERS

1. C – Stanley Morgan

2. B – 6,507

3. A – Wes Welker

4. B – Harold Jackson

5. C – 123

6. A – Wes Welker

7. D – Rob Gronkowski

8. B – Gino Cappelletti

9. B – Tennessee

10. D – Rob Gronkowski

11. D – Julian Edelman

12. C – 7th

13. B – Wes Welker

14. C – Marshall Thundering Herd

15. B – False

16. C – Rob Gronkowski

17. A – True

18. A – Randy Moss

19. D – 67

20. C – Ben Coates and Randy Moss

DID YOU KNOW?

1. Since being drafted by the New England Patriots in 2009, Julian Edelman has made one of the best receptions in the history of the Super Bowl, written children's books, and conducted the world-famous Boston Pops Orchestra.

2. Julian Edelman played quarterback for three seasons at Kent State. During his time with the Golden Flashes, Edelman passed for 4,997 yards and rushed for 2,483. However, the New England Patriots drafted Edelman in the 7th round of the 2009 NFL Draft to play wide receiver, where he has caught 599 passes for 6,507 yards and 36 touchdowns during his 11 seasons in the NFL.

3. Patriots wide receiver Mohamed Sanu Sr. was born in Sayreville, New Jersey, to a Muslim family and, as a child, lived in his parents' homeland of Sierra Leone, but eventually returned to play high school football in New Jersey and ultimately played at Rutgers University.

4. N'Keal Harry was drafted by the New England Patriots with the 32nd overall pick in the 1st round of the 2019 NFL Draft. Harry became the first wide receiver drafted in the 1st round by the New England Patriots during Bill Belichick's tenure and is the first wide receiver New England had drafted in the 1st round in the last 23 years, dating back to 1996 when they selected former Ohio State wide receiver Terry Glenn.

5. Patriots wide receiver Jacobi Meyers has been compared to Julian Edelman as both players transitioned from being quarterbacks in college to wide receivers at the NFL level. Meyers played for the North Carolina State Wolfpack as a quarterback, but following an injury, he was switched to wide receiver as the Wolfpack decided to start Jacoby Brissett at quarterback.

6. Although the number is commonly worn by receivers, no receiver for the New England Patriots has worn number 89. The Patriots retired the number shortly after Bob Dee retired. Dee was a defensive end for New England from 1957 through 1967. He was one of the first players signed by the then Boston Patriots in 1960 after playing two seasons for Washington and sitting out one to help tutor linemen at his alma mater Holy Cross.

7. The Patriots signed wide receiver Marqise Lee just prior to the 2020 NFL Draft. Both of his parents are deaf, and the wide receiver communicates with them through sign language. Although Lee sat out the 2018 season with an ACL injury and played sparingly during 2019, the Patriots like his experience and leadership qualities.

8. Randy Vataha was a wide receiver for the New England Patriots for six seasons after being drafted by the Los Angeles Rams in 1971, and signing with the Patriots as a free agent. He was reunited with his college teammate quarterback Jim Plunkett while playing with the Patriots. Vataha was a founding member of the United States

Football League in 1983, owning 50% of the Boston Breakers, and now he is president of a company that specializes in purchasing and selling professional sports teams.

9. Rob Gronkowski caught 79 touchdown passes thrown by Patriots quarterback Tom Brady, which represents 12 more than the next closest player for the Patriots. For his career, the tight end caught 521 passes for 7,861 yards while with the Patriots. Gronkowski has been reunited with Tom Brady as the two will suit up next season for the Tampa Bay Buccaneers.

10. Stanley Morgan holds the all-time pass receiving yardage record for the New England Patriots with 10,352 yards. However, Morgan is just 4th overall in career receptions for the Patriots with 534 or 128 fewer than team leader Wes Welker. Morgan averaged an amazing 19.4 yards per catch during his 13 seasons with the Patriots.

CHAPTER 5:

RUNNING WILD

QUIZ TIME!

1. Who is the all-time leading rusher for the New England Patriots, with 5,453 yards?

    a. Jim Nance
    b. Tony Collins
    c. Curtis Martin
    d. Sam Cunningham

2. What former New England Patriots running back leads the team in rushing touchdowns, with 45?

    a. Sam Cunningham
    b. Tony Collins
    c. Corey Dillon
    d. Jim Nance

3. What former New England running back holds the team's single-season record for rushing yardage, with 1,635?

    a. Curtis Martin
    b. Craig James

c. Corey Dillon

d. Jim Nance

4. In his rookie year, in 1995, Curtis Martin rushed for 1,487 yards and 14 touchdowns for the Patriots.

a. True

b. False

5. How many Super Bowls did Kevin Faulk win in his 13 seasons with the New England Patriots?

a. 1

b. 2

c. 3

d. 4

6. Patriots running back James White has gained 1,690 more yards receiving the ball than rushing the ball.

a. True

b. False

7. In how many seasons did Tony Collins score ten rushing touchdowns or more for New England?

a. 0

b. 1

c. 2

d. 3

8. How many rushing touchdowns did Curtis Martin have in his three seasons with the New England Patriots?

a. 30

b. 31

c. 32

d. 33

9. What former New England running back, with 2,500 or more career rushing yards, had the highest career yards per carry at 4.3?

    a. LeGarrette Blount

    b. Sam Cunningham

    c. Corey Dillon

    d. Kevin Faulk

10. From what country did Sony Michel's parents emigrate following the birth of his older sister?

    a. Jamaica

    b. Haiti

    c. Martinique

    d. Guadalupe

11. Former New England Patriots running back Craig James ran for the U.S. Senate for Texas in 2012 and won.

    a. True

    b. False

12. What former New England Patriots running back died in 2009 in a car accident at the age of 43?

    a. Robert Edwards

    b. Mack Herron

    c. John Stephens

    d. Sammy Morris

13. What university did Kevin Faulk attend before being drafted by the New England Patriots in 1999?

   a. Tennessee
   b. LSU
   c. Kentucky
   d. Georgia

14. What former New England Patriots running back won the Heisman Trophy in 1960 while playing for the Navy Midshipmen?

   a. Ernie Davis
   b. Bob Ferguson
   c. Joe Bellino
   d. Jimmy Saxton

15. What former New England Patriots running back leads the team in 1,000-yard rushing seasons, with three?

   a. Tony Collins
   b. Curtis Martin
   c. John Stephens
   d. Corey Dillon

16. The late John Stephens has a daughter Sloane Stephens who plays what professional sport?

   a. Tennis
   b. Soccer
   c. Basketball
   d. Volleyball

17. How many times has a New England running back rushed for 1,000 or more yards in one season?

    a. 14
    b. 15
    c. 16
    d. 17

18. What former Patriots quarterback leads the team in career rushing yards, with 2,176?

    a. Tom Ramsey
    b. Drew Bledsoe
    c. Tom Brady
    d. Steve Grogan

19. How many rushing touchdowns did LeGarrette Blount score in 2016 while rushing for 1,161 yards with New England?

    a. 18
    b. 19
    c. 20
    d. 21

20. How many yards is the longest run from scrimmage by a New England Patriots player?

    a. 80
    b. 85
    c. 90
    d. 95

QUIZ ANSWERS

1. D – Sam Cunningham

2. D – Jim Nance

3. C – Corey Dillon

4. A – True

5. C – 3

6. A – True

7. B – 1

8. C – 32

9. A – LaGarrette Blount

10. B – Haiti

11. B – False

12. C – John Stephens

13. B – LSU

14. C – Joe Bellino

15. B – Curtis Martin

16. A – Tennis

17. C – 16

18. D – Steve Grogan

19. A – 18

20. B – 85

DID YOU KNOW?

1. Corey Dillon set the New England Patriots' all-time single-season rushing record with 1,635 yards in 2004, averaging 4.7 yards a carry in scoring 12 touchdowns on the ground while playing just 15 of 16 games during the regular season.

2. Sam Cunningham played for the USC Trojans from 1970 through 1972 and formed part of the "all-black" backfield, which was the first of its kind in NCAA history for Division 1, that included quarterback Jimmy Jones and tailback Clarence Davis. Cunningham went on to become the all-time leading rusher for the Patriots and maintains that title today.

3. Curtis Martin rushed for 30 yards on his very first carry with the New England Patriots and finished the game with 102 yards, becoming the first New England rookie to ever rush for 100 yards in his debut. Martin finished the season with eight games of 100 yards rushing or more and led the AFC in rushing with 1,487 yards and 14 touchdowns.

4. Tony Collins was drafted by the New England Patriots in 1981 and was a Pro Bowl selection in 1983 as well as playing in Super Bowl XX for the Patriots that season. However, Collins suffered from an addiction to painkillers after an ankle injury, and that curtailed his NFL career.

5. Jim Nance was not selected until the 19th round by the

Boston Patriots in 1965 but ended up being a powerful fullback, rushing 299 times in 1966 for 1,458 yards and 11 touchdowns. Nance died at the age of 49 in 1999 after suffering a heart attack.

6. Sam Cunningham and Jim Nance are the only two players for the New England Patriots to have career rushing yardage of over 5,000 yards. Overall, only 33 players have rushed for over 1,000 yards in their career with the Patriots.

7. With 1,037 yards rushing in his Patriots career, Tom Brady ranks 33rd on the club's career rushing list but trails Steve Grogan, the leading rusher for New England as a quarterback, by over 1,000 yards as Grogan rushed for 2,176 during his stint with the Patriots.

8. Craig James rushed for 1,227 yards in the 1985-86 NFL season with the New England Patriots and was chosen to play in the Pro Bowl. That season, during Week 2, James caught a 91-yard touchdown pass, which was the longest touchdown from scrimmage in New England history at the time. James helped lead the Patriots that season to the Super Bowl, where they lost 46-10 to the Chicago Bears, and James gained just 1 yard rushing.

9. Kenjon Barner gifted his Super Bowl ring to his father on Father's Day in June of 2019. Barner played just five games for the Patriots in 2019, and despite a short time with the team, he was rewarded with a Super Bowl ring but opted to give it to his father.

10. Kevin Faulk is 5th in career rushing for the New England

Patriots with 3,607 yards but exceeded that total in receiving with 3,701 yards. Good enough for 13th all-time for the Patriots in receiving, making Faulk one of the best rushing/receiving running backs in franchise history.

CHAPTER 6:

IN THE TRENCHES

QUIZ TIME!

1. How many times was offensive lineman Bruce Armstrong named to the Pro Bowl for New England?

    a. 5

    b. 6

    c. 7

    d. 8

2. Offensive tackle Matt Light was named to three Pro Bowls, but how many All-Pro First Team honors did he earn?

    a. 1

    b. 2

    c. 3

    d. 4

3. Former offensive lineman Logan Mankins is only one of how many players on the Patriots named to six or more Pro Bowls?

    a. 6

    b. 7

    c. 8

    d. 9

4. Which former offensive guard for the Patriots has been considered the best offensive lineman in the history of the NFL?

    a. Logan Mankins

    b. Bruce Armstrong

    c. Matt Light

    d. John Hannah

5. How many straight Pro Bowls did left tackle Brian Holloway make during the mid-1980s for New England?

    a. 2

    b. 3

    c. 4

    d. 5

6. From what college was Dan Koppen drafted by New England in the 5th round of the 2003 NFL Draft?

    a. Connecticut

    b. Boston College

    c. North Carolina

    d. LSU

7. How tall was former Patriots offensive lineman Sebastian Vollmer?

    a. 6 feet 6 inches

    b. 6 feet 7 inches

    c. 6 feet 8 inches

    d. 6 feet 9 inches

8. Sam Adams Sr. played offensive guard for the New England Patriots between 1972 and 1980. What little-known university did Adams attend?

    a. Grand Canyon
    b. Prairie View A&M
    c. Presbyterian
    d. Southern

9. Former Patriots lineman Peter Brock played college football at what Pac-12 university as did his younger brother, who also played in the NFL?

    a. USC
    b. UCLA
    c. Arizona
    d. Colorado

10. Former offensive lineman Ryan Wendell played college football at Fresno State and was drafted by the Patriots in 2008.

    a. True
    b. False

11. How many games did defensive tackle Vince Wilfork play for New England in his 11 years with the Patriots?

    a. 157
    b. 158
    c. 160
    d. 161

12. Defensive end Richard Seymour was traded to what team by New England following the 2008 season?

    a. Oakland Raiders
    b. Washington Redskins
    c. Buffalo Bills
    d. Seattle Seahawks

13. Defensive lineman Bobby Hamilton collected 52 tackles, 7 sacks, and 5 batted passes during what season for New England?

    a. 2000
    b. 2001
    c. 2003
    d. 2004

14. Who played under the shadows of Richard Seymour and Vince Wilfork at defensive tackle for New England from 2003 through 2007 and missed just one out of 90 games during the regular season?

    a. Andre Tippett
    b. Ty Law
    c. Ty Warren
    d. Mike Vrabel

15. Defensive end Chandler Jones was drafted as the 21st overall pick in the 2012 NFL Draft out of what school?

    a. North Carolina
    b. South Carolina
    c. Syracuse
    d. Georgia

16. Former defensive end Chris Long played just one season for the Patriots during his 11-year career, and what year did he play for New England?

    a. 2015
    b. 2016
    c. 2017
    d. 2018

17. Despite playing just 14 games due to an injury defensive end, Andre Carter was one of how many New England Patriots selected to the 2012 NFL Pro Bowl?

    a. 11
    b. 12
    c. 13
    d. 8

18. Mark Anderson played just one season at defensive end for the Patriots but had how many sacks in the regular season and Super Bowl combined?

    a. 10.5
    b. 11.5
    c. 12.5
    d. 13.5

19. What former defensive end was undrafted in 2005 but signed by the Patriots after playing college football for Cincinnati?

    a. Jermaine Cunningham
    b. Mike Wright

c. Mark Anderson

d. Will Smith

20. Including the New England Patriots, how many teams did former defensive lineman Eric Moore play for in the NFL?

a. 3

b. 4

c. 5

d. 6

QUIZ ANSWERS

1. B – 6

2. A – 1

3. C – 8

4. D – John Hannah

5. B – 3

6. B – Boston College

7. C – 6 feet 8 inches

8. B – Prairie View A&M

9. D – Colorado

10. B – False

11. B – 158

12. A – Oakland Raiders

13. B – 2001

14. C – Ty Warren

15. C – Syracuse

16. B – 2016

17. D – 8

18. B – 11.5

19. B – Mike Wright

20. B – 4

DID YOU KNOW?

1. Willie McGinest holds the NFL record for the most career postseason quarterback sacks with 16 and the most sacks in any playoff game with 4.5. McGinest played linebacker for the Patriots from 1994 through the 2005 season.

2. Former Patriots cornerback and Hall-of-Famer Ty Law grew up in Aliquippa, Pennsylvania, and is one of 14 former or current NFL players to grow up in that city, including Darrelle Revis, Tony Dorsett, Sean Gilbert, and others.

3. Former Patriots linebacker Tedy Bruschi suffered a stroke in February of 2005 but went on to recover and play for three more seasons with New England before retiring and becoming an NFL analyst with ESPN in 2009 and was named the honorary captain for the February 1, 2015, Super Bowl XLIX.

4. Vince Wilfork played college football for the Miami Hurricanes before joining the New England Patriots. Wilfork was also a member of the Hurricanes track and field team and held the Miami indoor school record for the shot put until it was surpassed in 2013 by Isaiah Simmons.

5. Former Patriots defensive lineman Richard Seymour plays professional poker and has accumulated earnings of more than $600,000. At the 2019 World Series of Poker main event, Seymour took part and finished in 131st place.

6. Former Patriots defensive end Chandler Jones is from a very sports-minded family. Older brother Arthur Jones played in the NFL, while younger brother Jon Jones is the current UFC Light Heavyweight Champion of the World.

7. Julius Adams was the second for the Patriots defensive lineman in tackles during the 1982 NFL regular season with 45 and made one of New England's biggest plays of the season when blocking a field goal attempt by Miami's Uwe von Schamann in a 3-0 Patriots victory on December 12.

8. Former New England Patriots defensive end Tony McGee is the founder and host of Washington, D.C.'s, longest-running sports talk show that is minority-owned. The Pro Football Plus show has been airing for 35 seasons.

9. Ray "Sugar Bear" Hamilton was a defensive lineman for the New England Patriots from 1973 through 1981 and was the assistant defensive line coach for the Patriots the year New England played in Super Bowl XX.

10. New England traded up in the 2003 NFL Draft to select Ty Warren 13th overall because of how impressed Bill Belichick and his scouts were about Warren's college performance. Warren went on to play in each of the Patriots' 16 regular-season games his rookie season.

CHAPTER 7:

THE BACK SEVEN

QUIZ TIME!

1. What former New England Patriots cornerback was inducted into the NFL Hall of Fame in 1997?

    a. Raymond Clayborn
    b. Mike Haynes
    c. Ty Law
    d. Darrelle Revis

2. Former Patriots cornerback Ty Law led all NFL players in 1998 with how many interceptions?

    a. 7
    b. 8
    c. 9
    d. 10

3. Former Patriots linebacker Andre Tippett had 100 career quarterback sacks in how many games played?

    a. 151
    b. 152

c. 153

d. 154

4. How many seasons did Willie McGinest play linebacker/ defensive end for the New England Patriots?

   a. 10

   b. 11

   c. 12

   d. 13

5. In what year was former Patriots cornerback Ty Law inducted into the NFL Hall of Fame?

   a. 2017

   b. 2018

   c. 2019

   d. 2020

6. Former Patriots linebacker Tedy Bruschi won how many Super Bowls with New England?

   a. 3

   b. 4

   c. 5

   d. 6

7. Former cornerback Rodney Harrison played his final six seasons with New England. What team did Harrison play for in his first nine seasons in the NFL?

   a. Arizona Cardinals

   b. San Diego Chargers

   c. Oakland Raiders

   d. Buffalo Bills

8. Former Patriots linebacker Mike Vrabel is now the head coach of what NFL team?

    a. Baltimore Ravens
    b. Indianapolis Colts
    c. Houston Texans
    d. Tennessee Titans

9. Former Patriots linebacker Rob Ninkovich joined what television network in 2019 as an NFL analyst?

    a. CBS
    b. NBC
    c. ESPN
    d. FOX

10. How many BCS National Championships did Patriots linebacker Dont'a Hightower win while playing for the Alabama Crimson Tide?

    a. 2
    b. 3
    c. 4
    d. 5

11. After seven seasons with New England, what rival AFC East team did former cornerback Lawyer Milloy play with for four seasons before moving on to play for two other NFL teams?

    a. New York Jets
    b. Buffalo Bills
    c. Miami Dolphins
    d. New York Giants

12. Hall-of-Famer Mike Haynes played at what university before being drafted by the New England Patriots in 1976?

    a. Arizona
    b. California
    c. Texas
    d. Arizona State

13. In what country was Patriots cornerback Patrick Chung born?

    a. Barbados
    b. Jamaica
    c. Bahamas
    d. Trinidad and Tobago

14. At what university does the son of former Patriots cornerback Asante Samuel play?

    a. Arizona State
    b. Florida State
    c. Penn State
    d. Ohio State

15. Former Patriots linebacker Ted Johnson was an adjunct professor for two years in the Boston area.

    a. True
    b. False

16. Although known more for playing with Miami, what former linebacker started his career with the Patriots?

    a. Ted Johnson
    b. Nick Buoniconti

c. Kim Bokamper

d. Dick Anderson

17. How many NFL teams has Aqib Talib played for during his 13-year career?

    a. 3

    b. 4

    c. 5

    d. 6

18. How many former members of the Patriots defense are in the NFL Hall of Fame?

    a. 5

    b. 6

    c. 7

    d. 8

19. Junior Seau played for the New England Patriots for parts of six seasons.

    a. True

    b. False

20. How many seasons did Johnny Rembert play linebacker for the New England Patriots?

    a. 8

    b. 9

    c. 10

    d. 11

QUIZ ANSWERS

1. B – Mike Haynes

2. C – 9

3. A – 151

4. C – 12

5. C – 2019

6. A – 3

7. B – San Diego Chargers

8. D – Tennessee Titans

9. C – ESPN

10. A – 2

11. B – Buffalo Bills

12. D – Arizona State

13. B – Jamaica

14. B – Florida State

15. A – True

16. B – Nick Buoniconti

17. B – 4

18. A – 5

19. B – False

20. C – 10

DID YOU KNOW?

1. Rodney Harrison was voted twice by his NFL peers and once anonymously by NFC coaches as the NFL's "dirtiest player." During his NFL playing career, Harrison was fined over $200,000 and was suspended in 2002 following a helmet-to-helmet hit on Hall of Fame wide receiver Jerry Rice while Rice was playing for the Oakland Raiders.

2. Hall of Fame cornerback Mike Haynes finished his career with the New England Patriots with 28 interceptions after intercepting 19 passes in his first three seasons with the team. Haynes was named to six Pro Bowls during seven seasons with the Patriots.

3. Former Patriots cornerback Ty Law, who is now a member of the NFL Hall of Fame, was just five foot eleven but played a unique physical brand of cornerback and was able to deliver hard hits and bump receivers off their routes better than any other defensive player during his play.

4. NFL Hall-of-Famer and former linebacker for the New England Patriots Andre Tippett holds the New England all-time record for quarterback sacks with 100, including 65.5 sacks over a period of just five seasons equivalent to an average of 13 sacks per season.

5. Although Rodney Harrison only played six seasons with the Patriots, he is considered one of the best strong safeties

to not only play for the Patriots but also in NFL history. During the 2004 postseason, Harrison had four interceptions, of which two came during the Super Bowl against the Philadelphia Eagles.

6. Although former Patriots linebacker Willie McGinest has not played for nearly 15 seasons, the ex-outside linebacker holds the NFL record for most career quarterback sacks during the playoffs with 16 and played on three Super Bowl-winning teams while with the Patriots.

7. Current Tennessee Titans head coach Mike Vrabel excelled for the New England Patriots at sacking the quarterback, but the former linebacker also caught ten passes for the Patriots. All ten were for touchdowns, and Vrabel became the first defensive player to score a touchdown during the Super Bowl since 1986, when Chicago Bears defensive tackle William "Refrigerator" Perry did it versus the Patriots.

8. Devin McCourty was drafted in the 1st round of the 2010 NFL Draft by the New England Patriots after playing college football for Rutgers University in Piscataway, New Jersey, a school not known for its football prowess. Since being drafted, McCourty has gone to two Pro Bowls and helped New England win three Super Bowls.

9. Patriots linebacker Dont'a Hightower keeps a motivational saying taped to the inside of his locker below a picture of his mom L'Tanya and Morgan his girlfriend. The saying reads, "I cannot cry about having a lot on my plate when my goal was to eat."

10. The late Junior Seau announced his retirement at a press conference on August 14, 2006, but just four days later returned to football after signing a contract with the New England Patriots and started 10 of the next 11 games for New England before being put on injured reserve in late November. Seau signed with the Patriots again in 2007, as well as in 2008, and once again in 2009, but finally and officially retired on January 13, 2010.

CHAPTER 8:

AWARDS AND ODDS & ENDS

QUIZ TIME!

1. In what year were the Patriots awarded their franchise as the Boston Patriots?

    a. 1958

    b. 1959

    c. 1960

    d. 1961

2. The Patriots' overall record in the AFL was above .500.

    a. True

    b. False

3. How many Vince Lombardi Trophies have the Patriots won?

    a. 4

    b. 5

    c. 6

    d. 7

4. How many Super Bowls did the Patriots win in the 1990s?

    a. 0

    b. 1

    c. 2

    d. 3

5. How many AFC Championships have the Patriots won?

    a. 8

    b. 9

    c. 10

    d. 11

6. After playing their first Super Bowl in 1986, how many years passed before the Patriots returned to play in their second Super Bowl?

    a. 11

    b. 12

    c. 13

    d. 14

7. What team defeated the New England Patriots in Super Bowl XXXI in 1997?

    a. Dallas Cowboys

    b. Green Bay Packers

    c. San Francisco 49ers

    d. Chicago Bears

8. How many times has Tom Brady won the NFL MVP for the regular season?

    a. 3

    b. 4

c. 5

d. 6

9. How many times has Tom Brady been named to the Pro Bowl?

   a. 12

   b. 13

   c. 14

   d. 15

10. Who is the only Patriots player to win the AP Defensive Player of the Year Award?

   a. Mike Haynes

   b. Ty Law

   c. Andre Tippett

   d. Stephon Gilmore

11. How many players for the Patriots have won the AP Offensive Player of the Year Award?

   a. 1

   b. 2

   c. 3

   d. 4

12. By how many points did New England trail Atlanta in the third quarter of the Super Bowl before rallying to win?

   a. 23

   b. 24

   c. 25

   d. 26

13. What two players for the Patriots have won a Super Bowl MVP award besides Tom Brady?

    a. Deion Branch and Julian Edelman
    b. James White and Rob Gronkowski
    c. Rob Gronkowski and Julian Edelman
    d. Deion Branch and Ty Law

14. With four Super Bowl MVPs, Tom Brady has won more than any other NFL player.

    a. True
    b. False

15. Through 2019, the Patriots have played in how many consecutive postseasons?

    a. 9
    b. 10
    c. 11
    d. 12

16. Tom Brady is the all-time leader for playing in at least one playoff game in how many seasons?

    a. 14
    b. 15
    c. 16
    d. 17

17. How many New England wide receivers have rushed for a touchdown during the postseason?

    a. 0
    b. 1

c. 2

d. 3

18. Julian Edelman became the second Patriots wide receiver to throw a TD pass, catch a TD pass, and rush for a TD during the same season. Who was the other player?

    a. Randy Moss

    b. David Patten

    c. Deion Branch

    d. Troy Brown

19. What New England wide receiver has the second-most receiving yards in postseason history, with 1,442?

    a. Troy Brown

    b. Julian Edelman

    c. Deion Branch

    d. Rob Gronkowski

20. Patriots coach Bill Belichick has won how many Super Bowls with New England?

    a. 3

    b. 4

    c. 5

    d. 6

QUIZ ANSWERS

1. B – 1959

2. B – False

3. C – 6

4. A – 0

5. D – 11

6. A – 11

7. B – Green Bay Packers

8. A – 3

9. C – 14

10. D – Stephon Gilmore

11. A – 1

12. C – 25

13. A – Deion Branch and Julian Edelman

14. A – True

15. C – 11

16. D – 17

17. C – 2

18. B – David Patten

19. B – Julian Edelman

20. D – 6

DID YOU KNOW?

1. The New England Patriots have sold out every home game, including preseason, regular season, and playoffs, dating back to 1994 or 284 straight games as of the end of the 2019 regular season. The wait to receive season tickets is estimated to be between 12 and 13 years.

2. The Patriots played in the wildcard playoff game in 2019 for the first time since 2009 and lost at home to the Tennessee Titans 20-13. The loss was the first in the postseason at home for the Patriots since 2012.

3. Kenneth Sims was the 1st overall pick for the New England Patriots in the 1982 Draft out of Texas, but the defensive end played just eight seasons with the Patriots and collected just 17 sacks before retiring following the 1989 regular season.

4. Head coach Bill Belichick forfeited half of his salary the season the Patriots were caught in "Spygate" by videotaping a New York Jets practice. The Patriots lost their 1st round draft pick and went on to rout the Jets at the Meadowlands 36-14.

5. The rights to the name of Gillette Stadium were first held by CMGI.com prior to any New England Patriots game being played at the stadium, but CMGI.com went bankrupt and lost the rights, and the stadium was renamed Gillette Stadium.

6. Defensive end Richard Seymour played eight seasons with New England before being traded in 2009, but the outstanding pass rusher was also a fullback for the Patriots in many goal-line situations and was known as a formidable blocker.

7. Raymond Berry replaced Ron Meyer after eight games of the 1984 regular season as head coach and led the Patriots to Super Bowl XX the following season with an 11-5 regular-season record. New England lost Super Bowl XX to Chicago 46-10.

8. Current head coach Bill Belichick replaced Pete Carroll in 2000 after the Patriots had gone 8-8 in 1999 and 9-7 in 1998. Belichick did not start off well with New England as the Patriots were just 5-11 in his first season at the helm before improving to 11-5 and winning the Super Bowl the following season.

9. The Patriots have reached the postseason 27 times and appeared in 15 AFC Championship games, in which they have won 11. In the franchise's 60-year history, the Patriots have a regular-season record of 512-395-9, while their postseason record is 37-21-0 for an overall record of 549-416-9.

10. Tom Brady won seven MVP awards while playing 20 seasons for the Patriots, with three NFL MVP awards for his play during the regular season and four Super Bowl MVP awards.

CHAPTER 9:

NICKNAMES

QUIZ TIME!

1. What was the nickname of the 2019 linebacker corps of the Patriots?

   a. The Best
   b. The Boogeymen
   c. The PatPack
   d. The Linebacker Pack

2. What nickname was given the Patriots due to several cheating scandals?

   a. Cheaters
   b. Cheatscapes
   c. Cheatriots
   d. Cheatplays

3. What name has been associated with the Patriots dynasty during the 2000s due to Spygate and the hoodies coach Bill Belichick often uses?

   a. Evil Empire
   b. Cheating Empire

c. Evil Group

d. Evil Ones

4. The running backs for the Patriots during the 2017, 2018, and 2019 seasons were known as?

   a. The Three-Headed Monster

   b. The Four-Headed Monster

   c. The Headless Monster

   d. The Running Monster

5. The Patriots 2019 defensive secondary was called what after Jets quarterback Sam Darnold made a comment following a Monday Night Football game?

   a. The Stoppers

   b. The Gang

   c. The Ghosts

   d. The Tough Ones

6. What was New England's defense called during the Patriots' trips to Super Bowl XXXVIII and XXXIX?

   a. Homeland Defense

   b. Bend but Not Break Defense

   c. Unbeatable Defense

   d. No-Nonsense Defense

7. What were the poorly performing Patriots teams often referred to as?

   a. Poorsies

   b. Embarrassing

   c. Patsies

   d. Cream Puffs

8. What nickname did Tom Brady give Julian Edelman?

   a. Minitron
   b. Smalltron
   c. Receivertron
   d. Megatron

9. Patriots home stadium Gillette has been referred to by what name?

   a. Sharp
   b. Razor
   c. Shaver
   d. Facial

10. What name has been given to Bill Belichick due to Patriots scandals?

   a. Billygate
   b. Billgate
   c. Belichickgate
   d. Bill Belicheat

11. Bill Parcells was the head coach of the New England Patriots from 1993 to 1996. What was his nickname?

   a. Fish
   b. The Big Tuna
   c. Beast
   d. Porky

12. Sam Cunningham played running back for New England following a successful collegiate career with USC. What was Cunningham's nickname while with the Patriots?

a. Boomer

b. Blast

c. Bam

d. Buster

13. John Hannah is considered one of the NFL's all-time best offensive lineman. What was his nickname with the Patriots?

    a. Hog

    b. Hammerin

    c. Handful

    d. Blocker

14. BenJarvus Green-Ellis was given what nickname by his Patriots teammates because of the number of names in his first and last name?

    a. The Law Firm

    b. The Name Man

    c. Name Game

    d. The Doctor

15. ESPN commentator Chris Berman penned what nickname for former Patriots running back Curtis Martin?

    a. My Favorite Martin

    b. Mad

    c. Mow'em Down Martin

    d. Main Man

16. Tom Brady was given what nickname after winning his first three Super Bowls?

    a. Tom Boy

    b. Tom Winner

c. Tom Terrific

d. Tom Jones

17. Michael Hoomanawanui did not need a nickname with his unique name. What position did he play for the Patriots?

   a. Wide Receiver

   b. Running Back

   c. Tight End

   d. Offensive Tackle

18. What nickname was running back James White given while playing high school football for St. Thomas Aquinas?

   a. Quick Feet

   b. Quickness

   c. Sweet Feet

   d. Sweetwater

19. While playing with the New England Patriots, what nickname was Randy Moss given?

   a. Freak

   b. Downtown

   c. Middle Man

   d. Long Distance

20. While playing for the Patriots, Mosi Tatupu was given what nickname?

   a. Bulldog Samoan

   b. Snowin' Samoan

   c. Playful Samoan

   d. Strongman Samoan

QUIZ ANSWERS

1. B – The Boogeymen

2. C – Cheatriots

3. A – Evil Empire

4. B – The Four-Headed Monster

5. C – The Ghosts

6. A – Homeland Defense

7. C – Patsies

8. A – Minitron

9. B – Razor

10. D – Bill Belicheat

11. B – The Big Tuna

12. C – Bam

13. A – Hog

14. A – The Law Firm

15. A – My Favorite Martin

16. C – Tom Terrific

17. C – Tight End

18. C – Sweet Feet

19. A – Freak

20. B – Snowin' Samoan

DID YOU KNOW?

1. Russ Francis was an All-Pro tight end who played for the New England Patriots and San Francisco 49ers and caught 393 passes for 5,262 yards. While with the Patriots, Francis was given the nickname "All-World Tight End" by then sports announcer Howard Cosell, who was the lead announcer for Monday Night Football.

2. Ray "Sugar Bear" Hamilton was a defensive lineman with the Oklahoma Sooners and the New England Patriots. Sugar Bear was given to him as a nickname by classmates while attending Kennedy Junior High School as a teenager, and the nickname has remained to this day.

3. Gino Cappelletti played for the New England Patriots in the 1960s and was inducted into the AFL Hall of Fame. The running back, receiver, and kicker was affectionately nicknamed "The Duke" during his playing time in the AFL.

4. Gino Cappelletti played for the Patriots while Babe Parilli was the Patriots' quarterback. Parilli's pinpoint passes helped Cappelletti become the all-time leading scorer in the American Football League, and the quarterback / wide receiver relationship between the two was nicknamed "Grand Opera."

5. Leon Gray played for the New England Patriots, Houston Oilers, and New Orleans Saints in the NFL but was given his nickname of "Big Dog" while playing for Jackson State

University due to being 295 pounds at a time lineman often were no bigger than 230 to 250 pounds.

6. Former New England Patriots star wide receiver Stanley Morgan was drafted by the Patriots in the 1st round of the 1977 NFL Draft out of the University of Tennessee, where he was given the nickname "Stanley Steamer."

7. Kicker Adam Vinatieri currently plays for the Indianapolis Colts at the age of 47 and has won five Super Bowls, four with the New England Patriots and one with the Colts, and because of his excellent ability to make clutch field goals was given the appropriate nickname of "Iceman."

8. Willie McGinest played 15 seasons in the NFL after being drafted in the 1994 NFL Draft by the New England Patriots, but his nickname of "Willie Mac" was not as well-known as many other nicknames of professional athletes, especially those that had such a high-caliber career as did McGinest.

9. Patriots wide receiver Julian Edelman has been known to give his fellow teammates nicknames, and Malcolm Butler was no exception. Edelman described Butler as "strapping guys down" with his exceptional defense and therefore labeled his teammate as Malcolm "Strap" Butler.

10. Former Patriots defensive tackle Vince Wilfork was given the nickname "Air Wilfork" after the 6-foot, 325-pound lineman broke through the New York Jets line and blocked a field goal attempt by Nick Folk. Comparisons were then started between Air Wilfork and Air Jordan.

CHAPTER 10:

ALMA MATERS

QUIZ TIME!

1. Tom Brady played college football in the Big Ten Conference for what university?

    a. Michigan State

    b. Michigan

    c. Indiana

    d. Wisconsin

2. In 1971, the Patriots drafted quarterback Jim Plunkett who was the Rookie of the Year that same year and won two Super Bowls. What university did Plunkett attend before being drafted by the Patriots?

    a. Arizona State

    b. Arizona

    c. Stanford

    d. USC

3. New England Patriots linebacker Dont'a Hightower played for what college in the Southeastern Conference?

a. Tennessee

b. Georgia

c. LSU

d. Alabama

4. Doug Flutie played quarterback for the New England Patriots on two different occasions. The former signal-caller is best known for his Hail Mary passing completion against the University of Miami when he played for what team?

a. Virginia

b. Virginia Tech

c. Boston College

d. Holy Cross

5. Former running back Tony Collins played in the NFL for the New England Patriots and in Super Bowl XX. Collins played for what very small university before joining the Patriots?

a. East Carolina

b. Grambling

c. Southern

d. Middle Tennessee State

6. Tom Brady is one of just five quarterbacks in NFL and NCAA football history to win an NCAA Division 1 championship and a Super Bowl title.

a. True

b. False

7. Craig James, a former running back with the New England Patriots, said he decided to attend SMU, or Southern Methodist University, for what reason?

   a. He loved the football program.
   b. His girlfriend was enrolled at SMU.
   c. He wanted to play in Texas.
   d. He liked playing in Dallas.

8. How many games did Russ Francis play for the Oregon Ducks before transferring to Oregon State?

   a. 12
   b. 13
   c. 14
   d. 15

9. Former Patriots lineman Sebastian Vollmer was born in Germany and did not start playing football until the age of 14. What university did Vollmer attend before being drafted by the Patriots in 2009?

   a. Louisville
   b. Houston
   c. Berlin
   d. SMU

10. Steven Grogan played all his 16 seasons in the NFL with New England. What college did Grogan attend from 1972 to 1975?

   a. Kansas
   b. Kansas State

c. Wichita State

d. Missouri

11. After attending the University of Nebraska, Irving Fryar was chosen with what pick by the Patriots in 1984?

    a. 1st overall

    b. 2nd overall

    c. 1st, 2nd round

    d. 2nd, 2nd round

12. Corey Dillon played at the University of Washington before the NFL, but in how many junior colleges did Dillon play before enrolling with the Washington Huskies?

    a. 1

    b. 2

    c. 3

    d. 4

13. At what university was Terry Glenn a walk-on after selling soft drinks at the university's games as a teenager?

    a. Michigan State

    b. Kansas State

    c. Ohio State

    d. Iowa State

14. Chandler Jones played at Syracuse before being drafted by the New England Patriots. Jones's brother Jon Jones is a world champion in what sport?

    a. Boxing

    b. UFC

c. Karate

d. Judo

15. Sam Cunningham played 107 games for the Patriots and is the team's all-time leading rusher, with 5,453 yards. What college did Cunningham attend before being drafted by New England in 1973?

   a. Notre Dame

   b. UCLA

   c. USC

   d. LSU

16. Former Patriots wide receiver Deion Branch set a Liberty Bowl record in 2000 with ten catches for 170 yards and one TD for what university?

   a. Louisville

   b. Connecticut

   c. SMU

   d. Houston

17. Former Patriots linebacker Ted Johnson said he would receive a sheet of paper with the opposing team's audibles an hour prior to a game. What university did Johnson attend before being drafted by New England in 1995?

   a. USC

   b. Arizona

   c. Arizona State

   d. Colorado

18. What former linebacker for the Patriots played at the University of Tennessee and, following his NFL career, became the Patriots' inside linebacker coach in 2019?

    a. Ted Johnson
    b. Ted Bruschi
    c. Jerod Mayo
    d. Andre Tippett

19. Ronnie Lippett played linebacker for the New England Patriots from 1983-1991 after playing college at the University of Miami. Lippett intercepted 24 passes during his career with 7 thrown by what quarterback?

    a. Bob Griese
    b. Dan Marino
    c. Troy Aikman
    d. Bernie Kosar

20. Kicker Stephen Gostkowski played which two sports at Memphis State before being drafted by New England in 2006?

    a. Basketball and football
    b. Baseball and football
    c. Golf and football
    d. Tennis and football

QUIZ ANSWERS

1. B – Michigan

2. C – Stanford

3. D – Alabama

4. C – Boston College

5. A – East Carolina

6. A – True

7. B – His girlfriend was enrolled at SMU.

8. C – 14

9. B – Houston

10. B – Kansas State

11. A – 1st overall

12. B – 2

13. C – Ohio State

14. B – UFC

15. C – USC

16. A – Louisville

17. D – Colorado

18. C – Jerod Mayo

19. B – Dan Marino

20. B – Baseball and football

DID YOU KNOW?

1. Rob Gronkowski was named by rivals.com in sporting news as a freshman All-American while playing football for the University of Arizona before being drafted by the New England Patriots in the 2nd round of the 2010 Draft following his junior year, which he missed in its entirety due to having surgery on his back.

2. John Hannah was one of three Hannah brothers who played for the University of Alabama in the 1970s. Brothers Charley and David were also linemen voted to the SEC All-Conference team. Charley played in the NFL with the Tampa Bay Buccaneers and Los Angeles Raiders and was a member of the Raiders team that won Super Bowl XVIII.

3. Randy Moss signed a letter of intent to play for the Notre Dame Fighting Irish, and head coach Lou Holtz called Moss the best high school football player, but Moss was involved in a racially charged argument in high school that led to legal issues. Eventually, Notre Dame denied his enrollment application, and he ended up playing for the Marshall Thundering Herd.

4. At Arizona State, Mike Haynes was a two-time All-American and three-time All-Western Athletic Conference selection, ultimately being inducted to the College Football Hall of Fame in 2001. Using his quickness, speed, and

range to become one of the nation's premier collegiate defensive backs and an outstanding punt returner before being drafted by the New England Patriots in 1976.

5. Former Patriots kicker Adam Vinatieri attended South Dakota State University, where he lettered four years as the placekicker and punter and left SDSU as the football program's leading scorer at the time, with 185 points. However, Vinatieri, before South Dakota State, enrolled at the United States Military Academy but lasted just two weeks before dropping out.

6. Tom Brady was a quarterback for the University of Michigan from 1995 to 1999. He played backup during his first two years with the Wolverines behind future NFL quarterback Brian Griese and even at one time considered transferring to the University of California. Eventually, he became the starter in 1998 and 1999 and played every game for the Wolverines those two seasons.

7. Former Patriots linebacker Andre Tippett was a two-time All-Big Ten player while attending the University of Iowa as a defensive end. Tippett was also selected as an All-American and helped the Hawkeyes to their first winning season, the first title in the Big Ten, and first appearance in over two decades in the famed Rose Bowl.

8. Although Curtis Martin went on to become a five-time All-Pro in the NFL, his college days with the Pittsburgh Panthers were limited as he missed the final two games of his junior season. After playing one game in his senior

year, he sprained an ankle and missed the remainder of his final college season, and although he could have had a redshirt season to play one more year with the Pittsburgh Panthers, he opted to enter the NFL Draft.

9. Ty Law was on the cover of the Sports Illustrated October 3, 1994, issue, but not in a way he would choose to be. The photo shows University of Colorado wide receiver Michael Westbrook making a leaping catch over University of Michigan defensive back Law in the infamous play known as the "Miracle at Michigan."

10. Former New England Patriots offensive guard Stephen Neal attended Cal State-Bakersfield, where he was National Champion amateur and collegiate wrestler and a former world champion freestyle wrestler, but he is one of a handful players who played in the NFL who did not play football in college.

CHAPTER 11:

IN THE DRAFT ROOM

QUIZ TIME!

1. What player, who was a wide receiver for Arizona State, was the Patriots' 1st pick in the 2019 Draft?

    a. Braxton Berrios

    b. Malcolm Mitchell

    c. N'Keal Harry

    d. Devin Lucien

2. New England did not have a pick in the 1st round of the 2020 NFL Draft.

    a. True

    b. False

3. Jarrett Stidham is the new starting quarterback for the Patriots. In what round was Stidham drafted out of Auburn by the Patriots?

    a. 3rd

    b. 4th

    c. 5th

    d. 6th

4. Dont'a Hightower was the Patriots 1st pick in the 2012 NFL Draft.

    a. True
    b. False

5. With the 27th overall pick in the 2010 Draft, the New England Patriots drafted what defensive back from Rutgers University?

    a. Patrick Chung
    b. Devin McCourty
    c. Terrence Wheatley
    d. Jonathan Wilhite

6. In what round of the 2000 NFL Draft did the New England Patriots select quarterback Tom Brady?

    a. 4th
    b. 5th
    c. 6th
    d. 7th

7. In what year did the Patriots draft both Ty Law and Curtis Martin, who both are now in the NFL Hall of Fame?

    a. 1992
    b. 1993
    c. 1994
    d. 1995

8. In what draft did New England select Patrick Chung, Ron Brace, Darius Butler, and Sebastian Vollmer, all in the 2nd round?

a. 2009

b. 2010

c. 2011

d. 2012

9. Julian Edelman was drafted by the Patriots in 2009 after playing for what university?

a. Marshall

b. Ball State

c. Kent State

d. Buffalo

10. Patrick Chung was the Patriots 1st draft pick in 2009. In what country was Chung born?

a. United States

b. Canada

c. Jamaica

d. Brazil

11. What quarterback did New England select with their 1st pick in the 1971 NFL Draft?

a. Joe Montana

b. Jim Plunkett

c. Drew Bledsoe

d. Steve Grogan

12. How many times have the New England Patriots drafted 1st overall?

a. 5

b. 6

c. 7

d. 8

13. In 1984, the New England Patriots drafted wide receiver Irving Fryar with the 1st overall pick.

    a. True

    b. False

14. What defensive end did Bill Belichick draft with his 1st pick as head coach of New England in 2001?

    a. Jeff Marriot

    b. Dan Klecko

    c. Richard Seymour

    d. Ty Warren

15. What five-time Pro Bowler and two-time Super Bowl champion defensive tackle was not drafted by New England until 21st overall, after being considered a top 10 pick in 2004?

    a. Vince Wilfork

    b. Marquise Hill

    c. Richard Seymour

    d. Ty Warren

16. What conference did the first three picks for New England in 2018 play in?

    a. ACC

    b. Big Ten

    c. Big 12

    d. SEC

17. Which player was the first-ever player drafted by the Patriots in 1960?

    a. Tommy Mason
    b. Rip Hawkins
    c. Charley Long
    d. Ron Burton

18. In how many NFL Drafts has New England not had any picks?

    a. 0
    b. 3
    c. 6
    d. 7

19. In 1973, New England selected Sam "Bam" Cunningham from which university, 11th overall?

    a. UCLA
    b. Arizona
    c. USC
    d. Arizona State

20. Who did the New England Patriots draft 4th overall in 1973?

    a. Russ Francis
    b. John Hannah
    c. Darryl Stingley
    d. Mike Haynes

QUIZ ANSWERS

1. C – N'Keal Harry

2. A – True

3. B – 4th

4. B – False

5. B – Devin McCourty

6. C – 6th

7. D – 1995

8. A – 2009

9. C – Kent State

10. C – Jamaica

11. B – Jim Plunkett

12. A – 5

13. A – True

14. C – Richard Seymour

15. A – Vince Wilfork

16. D – SEC

17. D – Ron Burton

18. C – 6

19. C – USC

20. B – John Hannah

DID YOU KNOW?

1. Defensive lineman Richard Seymour who was chosen with the 6th overall pick in the 2001 NFL Draft by the New England Patriots, is considered the best 1st round pick made during the Bill Belichick era. Seymour was chosen for three consecutive All-Pro teams and played on the first three New England Patriots Super Bowl-winning teams.

2. Most football pundits consider former Patriots tight end Rob Gronkowski as the best 2nd round selection by New England. Gronkowski was chosen 42nd overall in the 2010 Draft and has been chosen as All-Pro, and he is now returning from retirement to play in 2020 with Tom Brady and the Tampa Bay Buccaneers.

3. The best late-round draft pick for the New England Patriots in franchise history is that of quarterback Tom Brady. Six quarterbacks were selected in the draft before New England took Brady during the 6th round of the 2000 Draft out of Michigan. Brady would go on to win a record six Super Bowl titles over a 20-season stint with the team.

4. The worst ever 1st round pick by the New England Patriots is considered to be defensive lineman Kenneth Sims who was chosen 1st overall in 1982 out of Texas but played in just 74 games over a period of eight seasons. The lineman made just 17 quarterback sacks and was eventually waived by the Patriots in 1990 after arriving at

training camp out of shape and following an arrest for drug possession.

5. The worst-ever 2nd round draft pick by the New England Patriots is considered to be cornerback Ras-I Dowling. The Patriots traded a 3rd round pick during 2010 in exchange for what turned out to be the 1st pick in the 2011 2nd round, and New England selected Dowling. The cornerback played in just nine games over the first two seasons of his career and made just ten tackles over that period and was cut by the team in 2013.

6. The Patriots at one time drafted defensive tackle Phil Olsen, who was the brother of Merlin Olsen, a former player with the Los Angeles Rams and a member of the NFL Hall of Fame. Phil was selected in the 4th round of the 1970 Draft but was hurt prior to the start of his first season with the team and never appeared in any game for the Patriots.

7. The Patriots have drafted a total of 11 quarterbacks since Bill Belichick took over as the head coach in 2000, including 6th round pick Tom Brady. The most recent quarterback selected was Jarrett Stidham in the 4th round of the 2019 Draft, and Stidham is now the starting quarterback for the Patriots in 2020.

8. New England drafted Jimmy Garoppolo out of Eastern Illinois in the 2nd round of the 2014 NFL Draft as the heir apparent to Tom Brady, but Brady played for another five seasons with the Patriots, and Garoppolo was traded away

during the 2018 regular season to the San Francisco 49ers and remained the starting quarterback of that NFC West team.

9. Quarterback Matt Cassel was selected by the Patriots in the 7th round of the 2005 NFL Draft, and Cassel covered for the injured Tom Brady following the first game of the 2008 regular season and led the Patriots to a record of 11-5, but Cassel was eventually traded in 2009 to the Kansas City Chiefs.

10. In the 2020 NFL Draft, the Patriots selected Kevin Asiasi from UCLA and Dalton Keene from Virginia Tech in the 3rd round with the 91st and 101st picks of the draft, making it the first time the Patriots have drafted two tight ends in the same round of the same NFL Draft.

CHAPTER 12:

THE TRADING POST

QUIZ TIME!

1. The New England Patriots traded for wide receiver Randy Moss during the 2007 NFL Draft. In what season did New England trade away the star wide receiver after he wore out his welcome?

    a. 2009
    b. 2010
    c. 2011
    d. 2012

2. In 2006, the New England Patriots traded away wide receiver Deion Branch to the Seattle Seahawks but reacquired the talented Branch during what season?

    a. 2010
    b. 2011
    c. 2012
    d. 2013

3. Former defensive lineman Richard Seymour was one of the most decorated players for the Patriots, but that did not prevent New England from trading Seymour in 2009 to what team?

    a. Kansas City Chiefs
    b. Denver Broncos
    c. Oakland Raiders
    d. Cleveland Browns

4. Prior to the start of what season did the New England Patriots trade quarterback Matt Cassel and linebacker Mike Vrabel to the Kansas City Chiefs for a pick in the 2nd round that eventually was used to select safety Patrick Chung?

    a. 2006
    b. 2007
    c. 2008
    d. 2009

5. In August of 2014, the Patriots shocked their fans by trading what offensive guard to the Tampa Bay Buccaneers prior to the start of the regular season?

    a. Tom Nelson
    b. Logan Mankins
    c. Rayfield Wright
    d. Leon Gray

6. During the 2001 Draft, the Patriots traded 39th, 50th, and 173rd picks in exchange for the 48th pick and used that to select what future Patriots Hall of Fame offensive lineman?

a. Matt Light

b. Logan Mankins

c. Leon Gray

d. Rob Gronkowski

7. In 2003, the Patriots traded Drew Bledsoe, Tebucky Jones, and three draft picks in exchange for how many players?

a. 4

b. 5

c. 6

d. 7

8. In October of 2016, the Patriots traded what player to Cleveland in exchange for a 2017 3rd round draft pick?

a. Sony Michel

b. Malcolm Butler

c. Jamie Collins

d. James White

9. Who did the Patriots receive from the Chicago Bears in exchange for a 4th round draft pick in 2003?

a. Andre Tippett

b. Raymond Clayborn

c. Corey Dillon

d. Ted Washington

10. The Patriots traded just a 4th round pick in 2013 to the Tampa Bay Buccaneers in exchange for what defensive back?

a. Malcolm Butler

b. Ty Law

   c. Aqib Talib

   d. John Lynch

11. In 2017, the Patriots traded quarterback Jacoby Brissett to the Indianapolis Colts in exchange for what player?

   a. Robert Turbin

   b. Trey Griffey

   c. Phillip Dorsett

   d. T.J. Green

12. In 2007, New England Patriots sent a 4th round draft pick to what team to acquire wide receiver, Randy Moss?

   a. Minnesota Vikings

   b. Oakland Raiders

   c. San Francisco 49ers

   d. Kansas City Chiefs

13. In 2018, the Patriots traded wide receiver Brandin Cooks for 1st and 6th round picks to what team?

   a. San Francisco 49ers

   b. Seattle Seahawks

   c. New Orleans Saints

   d. Los Angeles Rams

14. The Patriots traded a 2014 5th round draft pick to the Philadelphia Eagles in exchange for what defensive player?

   a. Isaac Sopoaga

   b. Fletcher Cox

   c. Cedric Thornton

   d. Bennie Logan

15. Who did New England draft in 2011 with the pick they received from trading Richard Seymour to the Oakland Raiders?

    a. Donald Thomas
    b. Dan Connolly
    c. Marcus Cannon
    d. Nate Solder

16. Who did the New England Patriots acquire from the Miami Dolphins in 2007 in exchange for 2nd and 7th round draft picks that same year?

    a. Ted Ginn
    b. Wes Welker
    c. Justin Peelle
    d. Chris Chambers

17. The Patriots gave away just a 2nd round draft pick to the Cincinnati Bengals in 2003 for what running back?

    a. Corey Dillon
    b. Antowain Smith
    c. Kevin Faulk
    d. Larry Centers

18. New England could have drafted Jerry Rice in 1985 with the 15th overall pick but traded that pick and one other to the San Francisco 49ers for three other draft picks.

    a. True
    b. False

19. New England traded a 5th round pick in the 2020 NFL Draft to acquire what defensive lineman from the Philadelphia Eagles?

    a. Michael Bennett
    b. Brandon Graham
    c. Josh Sweat
    d. Bruce Hector

20. New England acquired a 7th round draft pick from what team in exchange for tight end Jacob Hollister?

    a. Las Vegas Raiders
    b. Kansas City Chiefs
    c. Seattle Seahawks
    d. Arizona Cardinals

QUIZ ANSWERS

1. B – 2010

2. A – 2010

3. C – Oakland Raiders

4. D – 2009

5. B – Logan Mankins

6. A – Matt Light

7. C – 6

8. C – Jamie Collins

9. D – Ted Washington

10. C – Aqib Talib

11. C – Phillip Dorsett

12. B – Oakland Raiders

13. D – Los Angeles Rams

14. A – Isaac Sopoaga

15. D – Nate Solder

16. B – Wes Welker

17. A – Corey Dillon

18. B – False

19. A – Michael Bennett

20. C – Seattle Seahawks

DID YOU KNOW?

1. The Patriots had to give up just a 2nd round draft pick to acquire wide receiver Mohamed Sanu from the Atlanta Falcons. Sanu finished the 2019 season with 59 receptions for 520 yards and 2 touchdowns and is an important skill position player for the Patriots in 2020 and beyond.

2. Jamie Collins was unexpectedly traded by the Patriots in 2016 at the deadline to the Cleveland Browns with one explanation being he was ready to ask for money equivalent to top linebacker Von Miller, and the Patriots decided to trade him to another team in order to not have to pay a high salary.

3. In 2017, the Patriots made one of their most controversial trades when sending quarterback Jimmy Garoppolo to the San Francisco 49ers in exchange for a 2nd round pick. Garoppolo was injured after his first full season with the 49ers, tearing his ACL, but in 2019 helped lead the 49ers to a Super Bowl LIV appearance against the Kansas City Chiefs.

4. New England acquired safety Rodney Harrison in March of 2003 from the San Diego Padres, and Harrison immediately began terrorizing star quarterback Tom Brady during practices, which raised the intensity level of the team and helped him earn a captain's badge from happy head coach Bill Belichick.

5. In March of 2001, the Patriots signed linebacker Mike Vrabel who became an immediate hit for Coach Belichick as he was able to play multiple roles of inside and outside linebacker as well as defensive end and even played a few downs for the offense at tight end.

6. The Patriots acquired cornerback Aqib Talib in November 2012 from the Tampa Bay Buccaneers in exchange for a 4th round pick, but the biggest controversy was that, at the time of the draft, Talib was serving a four-game suspension. But as soon as he returned to the field, started shutting down opposing wide receivers for the Patriots.

7. In April 2007, the Patriots acquired veteran receiver, Randy Moss, from the Oakland Raiders in exchange for a 4th round pick, but several teams, such as the Green Bay Packers and Denver Broncos, opted not to trade for Moss. Personnel in Green Bay thought Moss could no longer run.

8. The Patriots traded a 1st round pick in 2000, a 4th round pick in 2001, and 7th round pick in 2001 for the New York Jets coach Bill Belichick, a 5th round pick in 2001, and a 7th round pick in 2002. Belichick to this day remains as the Patriots' head coach entering his 21st season, while out of all the draft picks the Jets received, only defensive lineman Shaun Ellis amounted to very much on the field.

9. In 2009, the Patriots traded a 3rd round pick to the Jaguars for a 7th round pick that same year and a 2nd round pick in 2010. In turn, the Jaguars were able to draft cornerback Derek Cox who played with Jacksonville for four seasons,

but the Patriots made out even better as the two draft picks they received in a deal were used to draft Julian Edelman and Rob Gronkowski.

10. Speaking of Rob Gronkowski, the Patriots wanted to acquire him before the Baltimore Ravens, who had the 43rd pick. New England came to an agreement with the Oakland Raiders to acquire the 42nd pick, one pick ahead of the Ravens, and ended up drafting the tight end before Baltimore.

CHAPTER 13:

SUPER BOWL SPECIAL

QUIZ TIME!

1. The New England Patriots have won the second most Super Bowls of all time.

    a. True

    b. False

2. How many Super Bowls have the Patriots played in?

    a. 8

    b. 9

    c. 10

    d. 11

3. How many Super Bowls titles has quarterback Tom Brady earned?

    a. 5

    b. 6

    c. 7

    d. 8

4. Tom Brady is 6-3 in Super Bowl appearances.

    a. True
    b. False

5. Only Tom Brady and what other NFL quarterback have won the Super Bowl in their first season as a starter?

    a. Brett Favre
    b. Peyton Manning
    c. Kurt Warner
    d. Drew Brees

6. Patriots quarterback Tony Eason was the first starting quarterback in Super Bowl history to not complete a pass, going 0 for 6 in Super XX.

    a. True
    b. False

7. How many Super Bowl appearances did former Patriots quarterback Drew Bledsoe make?

    a. 1
    b. 2
    c. 3
    d. 4

8. Randy Moss played in the Super Bowl for New England and Minnesota. How many Super Bowl rings did the wide receiver win?

    a. 0
    b. 1
    c. 2
    d. 3

9. John Hannah has been called the "Greatest Offensive Lineman of All Time." How many Super Bowls did he play in for New England?

    a. 0
    b. 1
    c. 2
    d. 3

10. Who intercepted a Russell Wilson pass in the end zone with 20 seconds to play to preserve the Patriots' Super Bowl XLIX victory over Seattle?

    a. Darrelle Revis
    b. Malcolm Butler
    c. Brandon Browner
    d. Logan Ryan

11. New England scored 25 straight points in the second half to tie and eventually win Super Bowl LI in overtime against what team?

    a. Seattle Seahawks
    b. New Orleans Saints
    c. Atlanta Falcons
    d. Los Angeles Rams

12. Former Patriots Chris Long and LeGarrette Blount are two of five players in NFL history to win back-to-back Super Bowls with different teams.

    a. True
    b. False

13. New England head coach Bill Belichick holds the record for most career Super Bowl appearances as a head or assistant coach with how many?

    a. 10
    b. 11
    c. 12
    d. 13

14. What former Patriots player holds the record for appearances as a kicker in a Super Bowl, with six?

    a. John Smith
    b. Stephen Gostkowski
    c. Adam Vinatieri
    d. Tom Blanton

15. What former running back for New England holds the all-time record for points scored in a single Super Bowl, with 20?

    a. James White
    b. Tony Collins
    c. Sony Michel
    d. Kevin Faulk

16. Tom Brady holds the Super Bowl record for most passing attempts, with how many?

    a. 389
    b. 390
    c. 391
    d. 392

17. In Super Bowl XLVI against the New York Giants, Tom Brady completed how many straight passes to set a Super Bowl record?

    a. 16
    b. 17
    c. 18
    d. 19

18. What former Patriots player holds the all-time Super Bowl record for receptions in one game, with 14?

    a. Randy Moss
    b. Stanley Morgan
    c. Wes Welker
    d. James White

19. Julian Edelman is tied for the Super Bowl lead for most career punt returns, with how many?

    a. 8
    b. 9
    c. 10
    d. 11

20. Adam Vinatieri and Stephen Gostkowski each hold the all-time Super Bowl record for career field goals, with how many?

    a. 4
    b. 5
    c. 6
    d. 7

QUIZ ANSWERS

1. B – False

2. D – 11

3. B – 6

4. A – True

5. C – Kurt Warner

6. A – True

7. B – 2

8. A – 0

9. B – 1

10. B – Malcolm Butler

11. C – Atlanta Falcons

12. A – True

13. C – 12

14. B – Stephen Gostkowski

15. A – James White

16. D – 392

17. A – 16

18. D – James White

19. A – 8

20. D – 7

DID YOU KNOW?

1. The New England Patriots scored 33 points in Super Bowl LII against the Philadelphia Eagles but lost nonetheless, 41-33, in a game in which the two teams also set NFL records for most yards gained by the two teams, with 1,151, and fewest punts for both teams during a Super Bowl, with one.

2. New England set the record for the fewest points scored by a winning team in Super Bowl history, with just 13, as they defeated the Los Angeles Rams in Super Bowl LIII by the score of 13-3. It also was the first Super Bowl where neither of the two teams scored a touchdown until the 4th quarter when the Patriots scored ten unanswered points to take the win after beginning the 4th quarter tied 3-3.

3. The Patriots not only have the largest comeback ever in a Super Bowl game after rallying from a 28-3 deficit to beat the Atlanta Falcons in Super Bowl LI, but also set the record for the largest comeback in the 4th quarter in that same Super Bowl rallying from a deficit of 28-9 by scoring 19 points over the final 15 minutes to send the game to overtime.

4. The Green Bay Packers and the New England Patriots combined to score the most points ever in the 1st quarter of the Super Bowl when New England outscored Green Bay 14-10 to open the first 15 minutes of Super Bowl XXXI.

5. The Patriots also combined to score the most points ever in the 4th quarter of a Super Bowl when New England was outscored by the Carolina Panthers in Super Bowl XXXVII, 19-18, during the final 15 minutes of play for a combined 37 points scored.

6. The New England Patriots lost to the Philadelphia Eagles 41-33 in Super Bowl LII, but it wasn't without a valiant effort, as the Patriots set an all-time Super Bowl record for net yards, rushing and passing, for a single Super Bowl, with 613.

7. Not all Super Bowl records are the kind that a team wants to have, and the New England Patriots are no exception. New England set the record for the fewest yards rushing in a Super Bowl after rushing for just seven net yards in Super Bowl XX against the Chicago Bears when beaten 46-10.

8. Thirty-five teams in Super Bowl history have not scored a rushing touchdown in a game, and the New England Patriots have the record for Super Bowls without a rushing touchdown, with four; the Oakland Raiders, Dallas Cowboys, and Miami Dolphins each have three Super Bowl appearances in which they did not score a rushing touchdown.

9. Although the New England Patriots were defeated by the Philadelphia Eagles in Super Bowl LII, the Patriots set the all-time record for most passing yards in a game with 500.

10. New England also holds the Super Bowl record for most

players with 100 receiving yards or more in the same game. Danny Amendola, Chris Hogan, and Rob Gronkowski had receiving yards of 152, 128, and 116, respectively, against the Eagles in Super Bowl LII.

CHAPTER 14:

THE FINAL QUARTER

QUIZ TIME!

1. When Tom Brady was drafted, he was the fourth quarterback on the Patriots depth chart. Who was #3?

    a. Drew Bledsoe

    b. Michael Bishop

    c. Steve Grogan

    d. Tony Eason

2. What player attended Notre Dame and played for the Boston Patriots from 1962-1968 before being traded to Miami?

    a. Babe Parilli

    b. Jim Nance

    c. Nick Buoniconti

    d. Ron Hall

3. Who was the head coach of the Patriots in 1990 when they finished the season 1-15?

    a. Raymond Berry

    b. Bill Parcells

    c. Rod Rust

    d. Chuck Fairbanks

4. What team beat the New England Patriots, 35-21, in Super Bowl XXXI in 1997?

    a. Dallas Cowboys

    b. Green Bay Packers

    c. Chicago Bears

    d. Minnesota Vikings

5. Which of these four quarterbacks was drafted 1st overall and played with the Patriots?

    a. Jim Plunkett

    b. Steve Grogan

    c. Tom Brady

    d. Doug Flutie

6. New England lost to the Chicago Bears, 46-10, in Super Bowl XX. Who scored the Patriots' only touchdown?

    a. Sam Cunningham

    b. Tony Eason

    c. Irving Fryar

    d. Stanley Morgan

7. By how many points did New England win Super Bowls XXXVI, XXXVIII, and XXXIX?

    a. 3

    b. 4

    c. 7

    d. 10

8. In what year was Tom Brady born?

   a. 1975
   b. 1976
   c. 1977
   d. 1978

9. How many times did Gino Cappelletti lead the AFC in scoring?

   a. 2
   b. 3
   c. 4
   d. 5

10. What team drafted New England quarterback Tom Brady in the Major League Baseball Draft of 1995?

   a. Chicago White Sox
   b. Boston Red Sox
   c. Montreal Expos
   d. Baltimore Orioles

11. What team did running back Corey Dillon play for prior to joining New England?

   a. Pittsburgh Steelers
   b. Cleveland Browns
   c. Baltimore Ravens
   d. Cincinnati Bengals

12. In which season did wide receiver Donté Stallworth play for New England?

   a. 2006
   b. 2007

c. 2009

d. 2010

13. What rule allowed New England to win against the Raiders in the 2001 postseason?

    a. The Roll Rule

    b. The Tuck Rule

    c. The Rattle Rule

    d. The Magic Rule

14. Which head coach led the Patriots to the playoffs in 1997 and 1998 but did not reach the Super Bowl?

    a. Pete Carroll

    b. Bill Belichick

    c. Bill Parcells

    d. Raymond Berry

15. During the 2003 and 2004 seasons, New England set a record season winning streak of how many games?

    a. 19

    b. 20

    c. 21

    d. 22

16. On October 31, 2004, the Patriots' winning streak that spanned the majority of two seasons was snapped by what team?

    a. Miami Dolphins

    b. Seattle Seahawks

    c. New York Jets

    d. Pittsburgh Steelers

17. Curtis Martin scored 37 touchdowns for New England, but how many did he score in his NFL career?

    a. 95
    b. 100
    c. 105
    d. 110

18. Who is the Patriots' all-time leading scorer, with 1,775 points?

    a. Adam Vinatieri
    b. John Smith
    c. Gino Cappelletti
    d. Stephen Gostkowski

19. Mike Haynes intercepted 46 passes during his NFL career, but how many were in a Patriots uniform?

    a. 28
    b. 29
    c. 30
    d. 31

20. Who is the only other player for the Patriots, besides Wes Welker, with 200 or more yards receiving in a single game?

    a. Terry Glenn
    b. Stanley Morgan
    c. Irving Fryar
    d. Randy Moss

QUIZ ANSWERS

1. B – Michael Bishop

2. C – Nick Buoniconti

3. C – Rod Rust

4. B – Green Bay Packers

5. A – Jim Plunkett

6. C – Irving Fryar

7. A – 3

8. C – 1977

9. D – 5

10. C – Montreal Expos

11. D – Cincinnati Bengals

12. B – 2007

13. B – The Tuck Rule

14. A – Pete Carroll

15. C – 21

16. D – Pittsburgh Steelers

17. B – 100

18. D – Stephen Gostkowski

19. A – 28

20. A – Terry Glenn

DID YOU KNOW?

1. Tom Brady is one of just two players in the history of the NFL to surpass 70,000 yards passing and 1,000 yards rushing during his 20-year career with the New England Patriots. Those numbers will increase as Brady has left the Patriots to play for the Tampa Bay Buccaneers for, at least, the 2020 season.

2. In 2001, former Patriots kicker Adam Vinatieri kicked a 45-yard field goal in a blinding snowstorm to help the Patriots win, and that kick is arguably the greatest in Vinatieri's career that continues today with the Indianapolis Colts.

3. Current owner Robert Kraft purchased the New England Patriots in 1994 for just $172 million, and as of the end of 2019, the New England Patriots franchise has an estimated value of $4.1 billion thanks in part to the Super Bowl victories and popularity of the Patriots around the United States and internationally.

4. Although the New England Patriots have won the most Super Bowls of any team in the NFL, with 6, and have played in the most Super Bowls overall, with 11, New England is just 4th overall in regular-season winning percentage at 56.1%, trailing the Dallas Cowboys, Chicago Bears, and Green Bay Packers.

5. Tom Brady finished his 20-year career with the New England Patriots with 74,571 yards passing, which is

number one overall for the franchise and is more passing yards than Drew Bledsoe, Steve Grogan, and Babe Parilli combined (73,090).

6. Rob Gronkowski is the second leading receiver all-time for the New England Patriots, with 7,861 yards, while Stanley Morgan is the all-time franchise leader, with 10,352 yards. Gronkowski is the only receiver in the top 5 of New England players who played tight end, while the other four are wide receivers.

7. The New England Patriots led all NFL teams with wins during the decade from 2010 to the end of the 2019 regular season, with 125 victories. Of those victories, 69 were home wins, which also led all the NFL during that period, and road victories were 56, which were also a league-high for the decade.

8. Not only have the Patriots led the NFL in regular-season victories, home victories, and road victories during the decade of 2010 through the end of the 2019 season, but the Patriots also led the NFL in points scored over that period with 4,720 points or 226 more than their closest competitor; the New Orleans Saints, with 4,494.

9. As of the start of the 2019 regular season, the New England Patriots had the most regular-season winning streaks of six games or more of any other team in the NFL since 2001, with 14. Tied for second best in that category are the Pittsburgh Steelers, Philadelphia Eagles, and Indianapolis Colts with a seven-game streak apiece over that period.

10. Dating back to 2001, the Patriots are first among all teams in the NFL regarding victories against playoff teams. The Patriots have won 63.6% of their games, 63-36, against playoff teams during that period. The second-best NFL team is the Pittsburgh Steelers at 48-58-1 or 45.3%.

CONCLUSION

There you have it, an amazing collection of Patriots trivia, information, and statistics at your fingertips! Regardless of how you fared on the quizzes, we hope you found this book entertaining, enlightening, and educational.

Ideally, you knew many of these details, but also learned a good deal more about the history of the New England Patriots, their players, coaches, management, and some of the quirky stories surrounding the team. If you got a little peek into the colorful details that make being a fan so much more enjoyable, then mission accomplished!

The good news is the trivia doesn't have to stop there! Spread the word. Challenge your fellow Patriots fans to see if they can do any better. Share some of the stories with the next generation to help them become New England supporters too.

If you are a big enough Patriots fan, consider creating your own quiz with some of the details you know that weren't presented here, and then test your friends to see if they can match your knowledge.

The New England Patriots are a storied franchise. They have a long history, with many periods of success and a few that were less than successful. They've had glorious superstars, iconic moments, hilarious tales, but most of all, they have wonderful, passionate fans. Thank you for being one of them.

Made in United States
North Haven, CT
06 December 2022

28042001R00075